RelationSHIT

theMKeffect

DEDICATION

For Baby Doll, with all my love

Contents

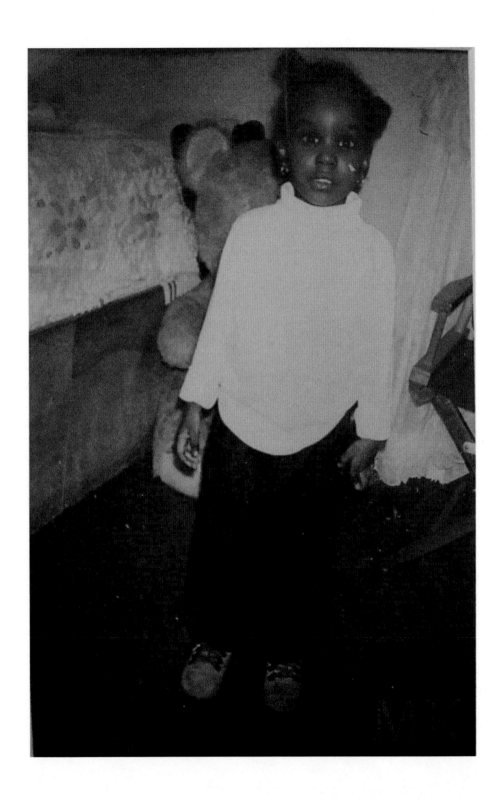

Acknowledgement

Dear Inner Child

You had a childhood marred with so much pain.

And I am sorry I could not rescue you.

Leaving you to be caught in a crossfire.

Drenched in the blood of others wounds.

Your innocence killed off too soon.

You deserved to experience the beauty of life.

With endless hugs and kisses

I am terribly sorry for all you had to endure.

You deserved so much more than what you got.

I promise you none of it was your fault.

And I hope that now you can see the light after the shadows of the dark

I will never leave you to embark on another journey alone.

Please forgive yourself for all you had to do to be you.

I love you Cella.

1 10.16.10

I can see a sadness in your eyes

To my surprise I don't understand how you don't realize how beautiful you are

I feel your pain I see your scars

I understand your struggles

How you try to juggle emotions between love and hate

Hoping that with me I can eliminate, not trying to intimidate

But I just want you to put your ill feelings to a demise

Wishing I could disguise your pain with my heart

I'm just letting you know that I can relate

So, I hope from me to you, you see that I'm trying to give you clues

That I'm willing to catch you if you fall

If at all you ever need me I hope you're not afraid to call

I just want to heal your heart and be there for you

2 FALSE PROPHETS

Instead of being loved at home

I was being loved up on by grown ass men that would pretend they loved me

Becoming a forbidden fruit that dangled before my eyes

It's no surprise that I became addicted to their connections

Somehow finding solace with these men between my thighs

Losing all control with my heels dug inside a mattress

Head sprung over the side

Vertigo

Caught up in a lustful blindness

To where the sex boosted my confidence and my ego

There is where I rode on a high that was hard for me to come down from

3 THE ENGLISH MAN

You were the first guy I met on the other side of love

And still til this day I will NEVER understand why you held me if you had every intention of letting me go

I wanted to call you

Often finding myself reaching for your phone number

Knowing I didn't have it, but wishing that I did

Oh, I wanted so much to tell you to come over

Wanting you to hold me just one last time in hope that it would feel like the first time

Realizing that if I did that, I'd be settling

It's crazy, my mind being so set on this fantasy of us being the people we once were when we first fell in love

Remembering every reason of how and why we began to feel that way

Those memories had become my crutch

Because once upon a time it felt like you completed me

And no matter how far we distanced away from each other somehow when I would get lost in the thoughts of you, you'd find me

Somewhere within letters or in songs

You were incredible in everyway

And sometimes, I hate that I still love you

But they say real love never goes astray

4 SITUATIONSHIPS

Oh us?

Oh no we're not together its complicated.

It's like we're together but we're not

NO labels, no emotions to this "thing"

We're just a fling

Oh no! I'm not looking for a ring

We're just fucking

It's getting cold outside so we're just cuffing

That's not my man, and I'm not his girl so basically we're nothing

We just go out on dates and stuff

Wasting each other time because neither of us know our worth

We know the truth but we don't want our bubbles burst

Afraid of being lonely in a snowstorm

Afraid that no one else will call

God forbid I be alone and lonely

Shit! I have needs

And he's so sweet when he calls

Sometimes I cook for him, and if he were in jail I'd probably put some money on his books

I just want someone to come and hold me

---

4 RelationSHIT

Stroke my hair, and console me

We're just talking mostly... about nothing, there's no future

And we're comfortable with that

We're friends, just friends nothing more exclusive than that

I know it's confusing it just doesn't make sense

But we're caught in this "thing"

And you know what I digress

And this is the type of love y'all want?

The "love" without a future

You'd rather lie and use your appendages to deny yourself of what love use to be

Thoughts of being cynical have been at the pinnacle of your disillusions

Hurt people hurt people, you know

Using your pussy as a weapon without discretion

Your pain disguised as power

And you just eat it up

Microwaved, shake and bake shit

Saying you don't want love so you settled for some fake shit

Neon pink dreams

Swimming in a river of each others creams

Lying there both sweaty in this euphoric falsehood of a romance

Excuse me if my feelings are ruthless,

But the truth is

If you ever end up wanting love that love could never stand a chance

Because you used yourself

Abused yourself

Digging yourself deeper into a pit

Situationships

I can't get use to that shit

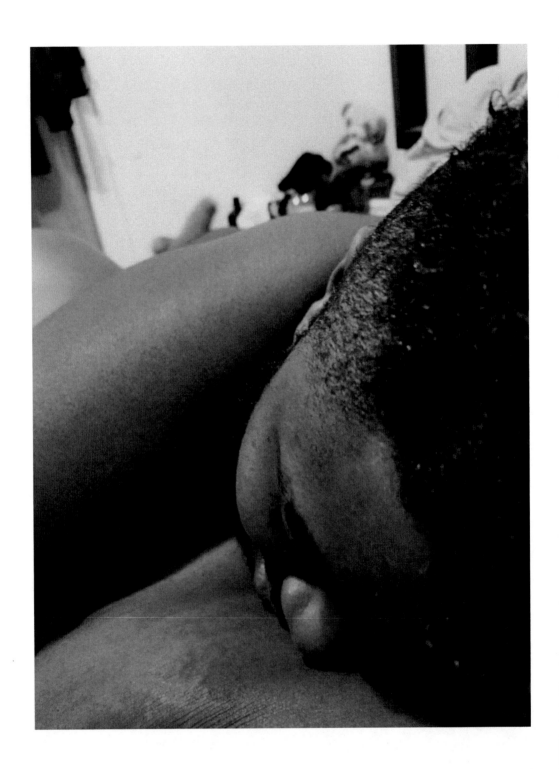

51.9.17

You were trying to seek the things you needed within yourself within her...

She gets it now.

The best thing for you to do to become the man you need to be to successfully love any woman is to leave her alone.

Let her find her greatness especially if you cannot love her properly.

The emotional tug of war of promising to change takes a toll on her heart.

It rips her soul apart and leaves her wondering and playing guessing games with herself.

She takes the blame because she thinks it is her.

Her mind goes into a tailspin trying to figure out what it is that she did wrong, and what she can do to fix it.

She changes.

She begins to stop loving herself trying to love you more, but you are too dumb to notice or to blind to care.

She's fading.

6 DATING AT 30

I have flirted with the idea of dating, but quickly realized that I had no interest.

I am too busy working on fixing my broken pieces so that the next I find myself dancing with the idea of being in love with a man he too has also come to peace with his brokenness.

7 AND... A PERSPECTIVE

Before you were my lover you were my brother

But I don't think any woman who lays down with the man she loves, and be-
comes pregnant wakes up thinking she's going to be raising that child all alone.
I would not wish single parenthood on my worst enemy.

And still through all this growth some days I still feel pain

Holding on to secret guilt and shame

And as she grows somehow she knows because my resentment shows

And for every question I try to answer with discretion trying to lend a hand to
help my baby understand that not everything in life goes as planned

And I try to understand why you still slight me to spite me even when I never
did a thing

But pray for you to win

But sometimes I wonder if you even give a fuck, if ever

Or, if you're just complacent with giving a few bucks

But you don't see that look upon her face

And you don't have to see her sadness everyday

Or hear her take the blame

And she's only three trying to deal with a real-world pain that you left me to
explain

And I can't just cover her void with my love

When you are suppose to protect her

Because you are her first protector

But what you show her is that the man she loves should neglect her and be emotionless

And you try to deceive by trying to be perceived that you're invested

When your only investment has been the presence of presents

But when is the last time you called?

And really been involved in her progress?

Or tried to help her process what has processed between me and you

And you think that buying presents means your around and present

And I used to feel sorry for your presence

But now I feel sorry that you're not present

And I used to feel sorry for your existence

But now I feel sorry that you don't exist

But the plot thickens when you think she won't remember the day you left the month before November

And I find it funny how history repeats itself

And how you left the way your father did

And the resentment that it ensued

But you pursued the same footsteps that you claimed that you would never do

And I admitted I hated you for that

And I regretted I dated you for that

And I hope you realize that the things you're missing have been vital

But you can't rewind the time

And I hope you're conscience doesn't eat away at you

As you travel coast to coast being a host for the country

Showing respect for a flag when you don't show enough respect for being a dad

RelationSHIT 11

And I pray that one day you'll show more love to your seed that you helped conceived

Because that has been the greatest love that I have ever received

And I hope when you finally realize that she's so great

It's not too late and she forgives you sooner than I did despite all the damage of what you haven't done

Love they say the many splendid thing

So many souls in need of searching

So many hearts left alone and broken

For love we have abandoned

For feast or famine

Because we have become so controlling and demanding

Leaving relationships before we examine what caused the break

We'd rather lie, cheat and steal before we reveal our scars

And it's so sad that so many dope souls will never come together

For lack of trust because we've concluded by creating illusions that love is fake, or we'll be damned if we get our hearts broken again and again

But if love conquers all then why don't we take a deep breath, exhale, and let love prevail?

9 11.13.17

Great girl becomes jaded, and she pretends jadedness is all she knew.

Tired of the over saturation and the under stimulation

So she fantasizes of the man she wishes she knew

And how he romanced her when he danced with her under the sweetness of the

Cherry moon

It was never my intention to inspire

Only my desire to ferociously walk through my truth truthfully with grace and dignity

I felt myself conforming so I had to start reforming to transform my former self

Because what I required was far beyond just earthly recognition

So, as I continued to align spiritually intentional every time

I was inclined to transcend into spaces with cosmic modality

11 WHAT THEY SAY

They say they love you

They say they miss you

They say they care

But those are just words anyway

Any I don't need words anyway

They say they can't live without you

Can't sleep, can't eat, can't breathe without you

But those are just words anyway

And I don't need words anyway

They say they want to marry

They say they want to carry

They say they want to hold you down and do whatever is necessary

But those are just words anyway

I wanted to believe so much that this time would be different

That this time you would follow through

That you would be the man you always promised me to be

But the difference never came

Chance after chance I gave you the tools to make my soul dance

And yet you still danced as if you had no rhythm

So there I stood alone in the middle of the dance floor without you as my part-
ner

Rather than to be swayed and sashayed around in the circles of complacency

You fooled me once, shame on you

You fooled me twice, and I sill loved you

But I'll never give you those chances again

13 3.24.19

Isn't it fucked up that I've got to act like I don't like you for the sake of not knowing if you like me too?

How juvenile is it for me to act like my feelings towards you don't exist because I fear the risk of being vulnerable and looking like a fool?

14 4.4.19

I know your intentions aren't pure

So, I ignore your advances

I'm not interested in giving chances for you to try and Jedi fuck my mind

I don't want to waste my time like that

So, I ignore your slick talk and smooth demeanor

15 Empath

They've all come to me for sanctuary

I'm considered a haven for lovers lost

A shelter to save hearts from a bitter cold

I've welcomed them with open arms an offer of my bosoms

Where they have laid upon to rest, and as they deeply sighed, I absorbed their energy inside my chest.

16 The Last of 31

Dear Marcella,

Your name means "WARRIOR" and I've watched you slay many dragons in pursuit of figuring out who you are live in such a way that has inspired others.

You are beautiful.

The intensity of the brightest star burning lightyears away.

The power of divinity, and the strength that is the Yin and Yang of the Sun and Moon.

You are incredible, and anyone that has had the privilege to be immersed in your presence within seconds knows your soul exudes the brightest hues of yellows, oranges, and reds.

You embody the Earth.

May you continue to embrace the changes, exhibiting the meaning of love of oneself, and others around you, and live out the peace you have always so desperately wanted.

You deserve life, love, and abundance.

I have watched you. I have loved you. I have grown with you. I am you!

Remember who you are, and why you have done your work.

You were meant to be here.

With great LOVE, PASSION, NOBILITY, HUMBLENESS, STRENGTH, and HONOR

Marcella, you are the shit!

With everything within me within you

I love you. I love me.

17 APOLOGIES NOT ACCEPTED

You're sorry all the time

You're sorry you couldn't make it

Sorry you had to leave

Sorry you didn't call

An ever-present collection of "I'm sorry" doesn't soften any blows at all

It doesn't change the matter that you didn't follow through, yet again

Your inconsistent action, empty broken promises and a bevy of excuses

All of which aren't doing this relationship any favors

Did you ever mean it?

Any of it?

Ever, at all?

And what the fuck do you suppose I do with them all anyway?

18 The Last of 32

Dear Marcella,

Here we are again celebrating another 365 days around the sun. You have only just begun to scratch the surface. 32 transitioning into 33 it's always bitter-sweet to say goodbye.

Look at you a Nubian incredibly Black Queen that sits atop a throne, embarking effortlessly into the abyss of the unknown.

You know I hype you up? But you deserve this shit!

Never forget WHO THE FUCK YOU ARE! You are the essence of your own planet. Vibes of the moon on its gravitational pull.

The world craves. Each year becoming richer in flavor like fine wine. I love the time you took to blossom, into this exotic flower.

Only dishing out what you want those to devour.

Sweet

Sour

Bitter

Salty

You are the umami of the Universe.

19 9.28.20

I was not birthed in love

My parents had a love for one another but were far from being in love

I was birthed into a home in which we did not honor ourselves

Nor each other

Devoid of emotions

Where we struggled and festered

Without speaking

Without listening

Just screams of chaos grounded in trepidation

Anger internalized

Hurt internalized

The inability to formulate tears for fear that I would not only be seen but heard

It was easy to be invisible

Fears that transitioned into PTSD

Disturbed by the imagery that has still haunted me

Of loud noises that triggered my insanity

Painstaking hardships of a weary spirit

Devalued allowing to be loved for less

20 5.24.20

Love letters

Conversations in song

Who knew that I could fall in love after so long?

What is more shameful?

What is more painful?

The time when you were nonexistent

We were close but we were distant

Ashamed I hadn't met you sooner

You a crooner to my heart

And as the love grows

We grow

And I'm not afraid or fearful

To have my partner, a man, my King

Where could I begin to hum the melodies to the songs you sing?

21 6.26.20

Sweet dreams and beautiful nightmares

I lie awake with emotions unfulfilled

My body still, yet conscious

Frost bitten from the chill of these cold sheets

I wish to lay upon you

Your warm body intertwined with mine

22 The Love of Rainstorms

The sound of the rain going pitter-pat on the windows

The rushing of wheels driving on the streets

An overflow of water pooling in the crevices of the sidewalk

The seepage of this rain delving into pores

Fuck long walks on the beach

I love taking long walks on the rain holding hands

So we can stop and suck the raindrops off each other's lips

23 DICKMATIZED

You know you shouldn't fuck with him

Because you don't have the trust in him

But that toxic dick feels good

Pussy talking to you screaming "YAS GIRL" you should

And he's talking to you real nice

He bites his lip, and with two grabs of that ass you don't even think twice

So, you fuck him, yes you did

That toxic dick comes fully equipped with six blank bullets in the chamber shooting at you with point blank range

The ability to cause instability

That toxic dick makes that pussy go insane

He gaslights, as you fucked all night and it was exciting

Enticing to the stupid parts of your brain

An influx of fast fucks

And when you fuck, and he busses his nut

It is as fast as he collapses wrapped all up in your pretty silky sheets

He wipes himself and greets you with a fast goodbye

Months go by without hearing from your "friend"

That dick goes ghost

Kick...

Push...

Coast...

His ego stroked feeding you visions of false hopes

And you eat it up

Going along with your temptations, leading you to

Sexual, physical, and emotional damnation

24 12.15.20

Don't love me first

Love yourself, love

So, I know when you're out here showing me love

You're coming from a place of love

And not simply searching for it

25 12.15.20*

I didn't even like to kiss

That was before I started kissing you and realized how soft and supple the sweet moisture of your lips made me cream

Kissing you made me feel like I was a cloud in my dreams

Floating like the effervescence of a soda pop

26 Elemental

Electrified with desire

They cast shadows just to be beside her

An essence of Yemeya and Oshun

She's unorthodox

She's out the box

She causes mass hysteria

Her aura gleaming, beaming like a blinding light

She's on fire like the sun and universally she smolders

So, as she catwalks they smile with toothy grins wolf whistling with mouths wet, and hung open, salivating hoping to cure their cravings

She's danger and as mysterious as the dark side of the moon

They want her, so they seek her like affirmations and powerful manifestations, like spiritual rituals of charging crystals under a full moon

They succumb

Falling at her mercy

As she becomes the puddle, the pond, the stream, the lake, and the ocean that quenches their thirst

27 The Man with the Yellow Aura

A man of Shamanic tendencies with eyes that read of Jasper

An aura burning bright of yellow hues

Medallion

Dandelion

And Bumble Bee

Cool and intrinsic like the color azul

Bassy like when B.B King would sing the blues

Loud like thunder when it first begins to rain

Soothing like silver when it covers our chocolate frames

Earthing in the reds of wines from the seven moons

I swoon, swept up in his rapture

28 FEMDOM

Duality of a switch-hitting personality

Black magic dungeon style vibes

Secret safe words only shared between you and I

Devotions of pleasure explosions

A sexual prowess

Provocative manner

In dark rooms full of paddles and chains

Come here my little submissive, and let me fuck the soul up out your frame

Red lights, strobe lights

Candlewax tribbing on my dinner

Open wide and let me suck every ounce of cum from your innards

Loud screams and belly moans from satiated windpipes

Sensations from pleasurable orgasmic conversations

No hesitations or reservations

As you black out from gasping for some air

I told you, you were my bitch tonight, so enter if you dare

29 Mirrored LOVE

It wasn't until I started to hold the mirror up to myself did, I   begin
to realize

That the love I wanted had to begin and end with me

And when I did, I knew I was not about to roam the Earth with the lures
of my past leading the way

They say love begets love

And here I was saturating absolutely everything in my path
with it

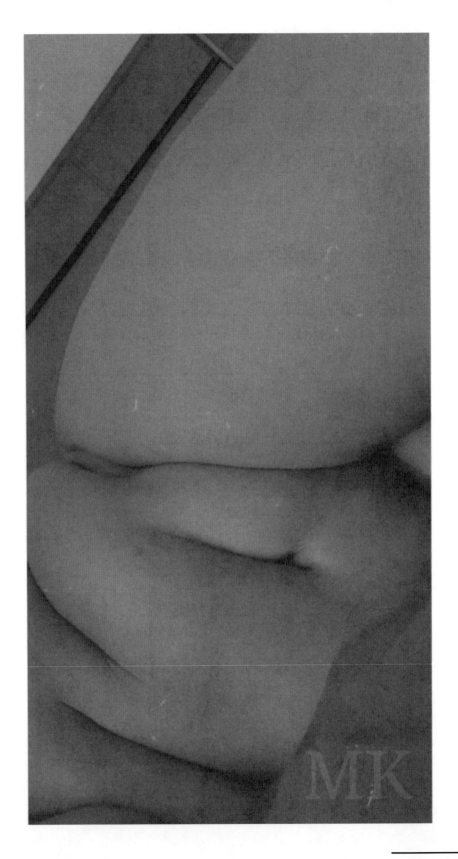

30 Fupa LOVE

Soft place belly rubs

In the thick of it I love

Warmth when touching me

31 SHAKESPEARE

I want to see you

I want to do nothing more than to run into your arms and be in your presence at this precise moment

To feel you

To bask in your energy for a long as we both desire to be there

I've missed you severely

Seconds into minutes

Minutes into hours

Hours turning into days that turn into weeks since we've last laid eyes on one another

Just the mere thought of being away from you any longer crushes me

Longing, longing only wanting my lips to be so firmly pressed upon yours

When will I see you?

32 REFLECTION

What do you see when you look at me?

I see all you are BE.COMING

For yourself

For your family

For your goals

For the legacy you wish to leave behind

I see a woman that was once set off in fear and trepidation enter the unknown with charm, conviction, and solidarity

I want to mirror you

Inspired, constantly in awe of how you move optimistically fluid in your life

50 RelationSHIT

33 838 WASHINGTON ST

I came from brokenness

With anger that erupted like volcanos spewing lava

A courtship driven from hell and full of drama

Doused like fire filled with trauma

I felt like I was living proof that there was karma

With spirits brown and drowned from sound

A darkness that lingered in the corners of dark hallways and underneath the stairs

In my bedroom with the door shut staying away from my living hell

A hot pink desk that anchored my room where I'd sit and write all day

Singing songs that blared from my radio just to wash my tears away

Where my mattress reminded me daily of galaxies far and furthest away

My escape into the reclusion that was in between the pages of dusty books

Where highlighters became my only sunshine

Outside feeling like fresh out of jail

My bike being my vehicle that took me to any and everyplace

Laughter being the mask behind the sadness that they confused with being resting bitch face

My silence often mistaken for being shy

Crying and the burning of an acid cry

Afraid to speak fearing they'd hear the truth inside my voice

Lying for a reason feeling that I had no choice

34 THE LAST OF 33

Dear Marcella,

33 years you have survived yet this last year you have seemed to bloom in front of the world's eyes.

People who hadn't noticed you before have begun to notice you.

People that tried to count you out have realized that was mistake.

Your energy presenting itself in rooms before you do.

I know it took you a long time to get here, but I am so delighted that you have finally reached your mountain top and can finally see what you have always had inside.

Like I always tell you 'YOU ARE THE SHIT'

This year alone you have thrived crushing every single goal you set out for

This is your season to be celebrated, honored, and exponentially loved.

You never cease to amaze me. With all that you could have been due to your circumstances, but you chose to forge a greater path.

Your thoughtfulness, your capacity to care for others even when you are in the darkest parts of your own storms.

I have always admired you and your ability to understand the misunderstood.

cues Nina Simone's Don't Let Me Be Misunderstood

You deserve everything you have always dreamed of.

You are the light.

I encourage you to continue to heal, to grow, to thrive, to forgive, to love, to inspire, and most importantly LIVE!

The world deserves you, as you are unlike anything this planet has ever seen.

I love you.

ABOUT THE AUTHOR

theMKeffect is an artist residing in Boston, Ma. She uses different elements of art to showcase her love of sexuality, spirituality, body positivity, and love. In her writings she hopes to inspire others to embrace themselves. She believes in living authentically and saying "fuck the status quo. To learn more about her and support her art you can check her out on the following platforms.

www.themkeffect.com

Instagram at @themkeffect @myheartyourstomach @themoodexperience

Snapchat @themkeffect

Made in the USA
Middletown, DE
21 September 2023

38960245R00035